# Practical Business Marketing and Advertising Strategies:

*How you can successfully market and advertise your business using platforms like affiliate marketing, LinkedIn, Twitter, Facebook, and blogging*

By Calvin Kennedy

©WE CANT BE BEAT LLC

# Table of Contents

Introduction .................................................................. 6

Chapter 1: Email marketing and advertising ............. 10

1.1 Basics of Email Marketing For New Marketers ................................................................... 10

1.2 Why should you make use of email marketing? ................................................................... 11

1.3 What are the disadvantages of email marketing? .................................................................. 11

1.4 Email Marketing Strategies ............................... 13

1.5 Is Email Marketing Right for Your Business? . 21

1.6 Writing Emails That Are More Effective .......... 26

1.7 Email Address List for email marketing .......... 28

1.8 Email Marketing Software and its Benefits ..... 30

Chapter 2: Social Media marketing and advertising 34

2.1 What Exactly Is Social Media? .......................... 34

2.2 Do You Need Social Media? ............................... 36

2.3 Blogs ................................................................... 38

What Are Blogs? ........................................... 38

Components of A Blog ................................... 40

Steps To Develop Your Blog ......................... 43

Free Blog Marketing Tips ............................ 46

2.4 Facebook ............................................................ 50

What is Facebook? ...................................... 50

What makes Facebook an important
marketing platform? ................................... 51

2.5 LinkedIn ................................................. 53

What is LinkedIn? ...................................... 53

Tips on getting started ............................... 54

LinkedIn Marketing ................................... 56

2.6 Twitter ..................................................... 59

What is Twitter and Twitter Marketing? ... 59

Tips to Using Twitter .................................. 62

2.7 Instagram ................................................ 66

What is Instagram ...................................... 66

Ways of gaining Instagram Followers ....... 66

2.8 Social Media Marketing Tools for Your
Business ....................................................... 70

2.9 Social Media Promotion Don'ts .......... 75

Chapter 3: Affiliate marketing .................... 79

3.1 What Is Affiliate Marketing and How Does It
Work For Me? ............................................. 79

3.2 Affiliate Marketing Tips - How to Find a Niche
Market ......................................................... 83

3.3 Drawing Quality Targeted Users to Your
Website, Fast! ............................................. 87

3.4 Tips to create High Traffic Website Growth ... 89

3.5 How To Get High-Quality Backlinks ............... 93

Chapter 4: Brand Building Strategy.............................98

Conclusion...................................................................101

# Introduction

The internet has truly become the most important technological advancement in the history of the world. The internet connects billions of people, businesses, institutions and governments around the globe. With this development came the emergence of E-commerce. This means that a considerable number of business transactions are already done online. As such, there will be businesses that will need to advertise on the internet to promote their goods and services. In the traditional sense of the word, advertising means advertisements in newspapers, magazines, posters and other tangible materials. However, in online marketing, everything is done in cyberspace.

In affiliate marketing, not only is the advertisement done online but also businessmen who need the advertisement will only pay based on the performance of such advertisement. As such, affiliate marketing is a form of performance-based marketing.

In the internet, traditional online advertisements can come in a lot of ways. For example, businesses are normally asked to pay a fixed rate for each advertisement space they virtually 'lease' on the internet. This virtual space includes banner ads on websites and other web blogs. The problem with this system is that the business will be required to pay a fixed fee regardless of the performance of the ad. With affiliate marketing, the exposure of an ad is certain. However, the difference between affiliate marketing ads and the usual traditional online ads is that the business will only pay for the former when an action by a visitor and/or prospective client is done. This action may include clicking the ad, ordering the product or service outright, or simply filling out some forms. The payment for the affiliate can be thought of as a 'commission.' Therefore, if there is no effect or action by a visitor or prospective client, the business will not pay the affiliate.

This is a win-win situation for both the business and the affiliate. First, the business will only pay when there is performance. Second, the affiliate will be motivated to come up with strategies and techniques that will enhance the chances that a visitor or prospective client will perform an action. Third, there is no limit on what the affiliate can earn (as opposed to the traditional online space ad fixed rate) because the better the performance of his ads, the more earnings he will make.

The business refers to the company, firm or organization that has the intention to sell a product, good, commodity or service. In other words, the business is essentially a merchant. This means that he will pay the affiliate for the marketing that he or she does to promote the purchase of his product, good, commodity or service.

Affiliate, on the other hand, refers to the owner or blogger of a specified business website or blog that is allowed by a business to advertise on its behalf. It is fervently hoped by the author that you, the reader, will earn income from the internet through reading and rereading this work and consistently applying the proven techniques, strategies and methods outlined in this book.

Thanks for purchasing this book. It's my firm belief that it will provide you with all the answers to your questions.

# Chapter 1: Email marketing and advertising

## 1.1 Basics of Email Marketing For New Marketers

Email marketing is an efficient way of distributing information about a product or service. This direct marketing method makes use of a fast and effective tool: electronic mail. The main issue that usually shakes the identity of such a method is its association with spamming. Spamming is what some people would consider an underhanded version of email marketing. Companies, without asking permission from potential clients or buyers, bombard said clients' email addresses with information about products and services. Sometimes spammed email contains links to fraudulent websites that the client would not want to be associated with. Instead of just reminding the email recipients, spammers bombard the poor targets with all sorts of unwanted information. As a result, would-be customers feel that their privacy has been invaded.

## 1.2 Why should you make use of email marketing?

When you use email to inform possible clients about your products and services, you do not have to go to the post office and send a bulk of letters. This means you do not have to spend money on printing or postage, both of which can cost a lot. Advertising your company through email makes the whole advertising process so much faster and more efficient. You can reach more people in a short period of time. If you happen to have a quality mailing list of people, who have requested to receive your emails, you can benefit by promoting your existing products and build a stronger relationship with them. You can run special promotions during the holidays or another seasonal event without requiring a lot of lead time.

## 1.3 What are the disadvantages of email marketing?

The problem with the technique is that many Internet users are wary of the email from companies; although recent studies indicate that the majority of people are becoming more comfortable with the idea. Email has been known to be a medium for spamming and viruses. Would-be clients are becoming more careful about the mail that they open, which is why it is so important that you clearly identify yourself in the from name of your emails. If the recipients of the email are not familiar with your company or does not recognize the company name, then they may not even open your email. This results in your effort becoming useless. At times, the email recipients do not even get a glimpse of your email if it seems foreign to them. With all sorts of email filters available today, your unrecognized email could be directly sent to the spam box. There may be recipients who do open the mail but do not take your correspondence seriously. They have not really heard of you before your email came into their inbox. They are also more likely wondering how you got their email address. This is why building a quality permission-based mailing list is vital to your email marketing success.

Email marketing, in general, still delivers great results and is one of the most rapidly growing marketing tools. It is fast, cheap and efficient. You get to spread the word about your company's products and services in almost no time. With one click, your email is sent to possibly hundreds, thousands or even more. Your contacts can also get connected to your online shop through a link within the email. This way, they can buy the product in as few steps as possible, which is exactly what you want.

## 1.4 Email Marketing Strategies

Many marketers and traders are aware of the effectiveness and application of email marketing strategies and how one such strategy can reach out to an unlimited number of people in the shortest amount of time.

Businesses especially dealing with sales and marketing require the best means to find customers to sustain their company's money flow and transactions. The use of email marketing strategies allow companies and online based shops and stores to target a variety of people and customers using the simplest yet most effective avenue for connectivity, the Internet.

Just years ago, thousands of shops and malls had been closed due to the lack of innovation and progress in their business methodology. The ones, which have survived can attribute their continued success to the Internet's ability to give information and data regarding their products to an unlimited number of people without spending a fortune on their sales campaign.

In fact, a comparative study has been conducted by several universities to examine and evaluate the effects of the Internet in one's business. As expected, businesses equipped with the Internet which specifically allowed them to use email marketing strategies were the ones that performed better and more effectively.

Because of this, many businessmen, company presidents, and CEO's have dedicated a lot of their resources to the establishment of effective email marketing strategies. The method of advertisement using this online medium is very simple yet has a gigantic impact on increased company performance. This is because the only requirement is to have an affiliation with electronic mail servers providers, which would cost less compared to hiring a team of professional marketers and campaign managers. The fees would differ by at least thousands of dollars. Once an affiliation has been integrated with the email authorities, marketers can create advertisements and commercials which can be easily included in message boards which can be easily seen by millions of people at a time.

Through the email marketing strategies, people can easily track down their potential clients using their connectivity with other online stores in which they have a membership with. The customer profile and tendency of a buyer can be predicted using his Internet activities, which can be summed up in one's membership in a specific kind of websites. This is the main point considered by marketers when targeting a specific person to participate in the email marketing strategies.

People who have accounts on model-based sites are the ones usually being targeted by marketers of fashion products using the email marketing strategies. Emails regarding the latest and up to date items would be constantly sent to the target customer. Since the marketer has affiliations with the electronic mail company, they could send out invitations and advertisements to the people on this person's list of friends and acquaintances. The chances that the person shares the same interest with his friends are high, which would increase the eliciting of a favorable response. This is why email marketing strategies are considered one of the best means to increase your business' profits.

## Choose, grow and develop your email marketing data list

Building and growing a targeted email database can be tough at the beginning. You should have a list of existing customer's emails to market to. Expand this by asking them to recommend or send to a friend. Opening new marketing channels, using a data company can provide an email address. Leigh Cooke Southampton says it is important to work closely with the data provider and be specific on your data needs.

## Clean and segmented email marketing database

Regular data cleansing of your email marketing list means removing customers who have opted out of emails from you. By having a quality email, marketing database then allows you to target your messages. If your database is large enough - segmenting the email market will further focus your message and offer greater email marketing success. Segmentation may be by location, profession, age, new or repeat customers.

Formatting your email

Here are a few email marketing tips to ensure they get to your target's inbox.

Rich text (HTML) and plain text emails

Some email clients will allow for rich text emails or HTML emails - this is where you can use different fonts, images, hyperlinks and color in your email. Plain text emails, is where the email is in its most basic form - just words! Plain text may be more prevalent on mobile devices - where people may read emails on the way to work. Whether it is rich text or plain text - the content writer should offer a compelling copy to keep the reader interested. Another option for plain text emails - is also to offer a landing page for HTML readers to use. Leigh Cooke Southampton says it is important not to assume the reader will copy and paste the link to another website page. Therefore, the copy should attract their attention in the first instance.

Email marketing links

Using links in rich text emails allows readers to be directed to the product or service you are discussing. Professional copywriter follows a simple rule of thumb - one link per paragraph. We all know that too many links look cluttered. However, not enough email links reduce click through rates.

Email layout

The email client, your customers, use, may not be the same as yours. Therefore - do not assume the way it looks on your screen, is how it will look in others. Some email CRM systems allow you to view popular email client layouts. Choose fonts and sizes that are consistent throughout - such as Tahoma, Calibre or Times New Roman.

Consistency and company branding

Keep your emails consistent - use the same formatting, layout, and colors. Readers like continuity and familiarity when reading emails. Keeping the colors and fonts of the brand help readers make that connection with the email, website, and company.

What's your email spam score?

-Avoid spam words - 'free', 'save', '£', 'discount' e.t.c

-Avoid spam colors - reds and yellows

-Avoid spam tables and images - too many will be classed as spam.

Personalize your email

Email marketing personalisation is great for conversion rates. Where possible, address the reader with their first or last name in email marketing. Readers will not feel like a number with their name in the email, and are therefore more likely to keep reading and act.

One message in the email campaign

Stick to one message per email. Too many messages will discourage any reading; therefore, the email will end up in the 'deleted' folder! Keep the key message in the subject line and first few lines of the email - so the readers just skimming the email will get the message. Leigh Cooke Southampton suggests this is a bit more flexible for company newsletters - a maximum of 3 messages.

Strong call to action

Email marketing needs a strong call to action. Try and place the call to action at the top, middle and bottom of the email copy. Call to actions may include email, completing a form, downloading a white paper, calling the sales team or just visiting your website for more information. Choose one call to action and make it visible.

Proofread your email marketing campaigns

Proofing read your email marketing copy is essential. Whether it's yourself, your boss or a colleague in another department - a fresh pair of eyes should be able to:

-Instantly know what is on offer - one message

-Easily scan and read the email - good formatting

-Find any spelling or grammatical errors - 100% perfect

-Know what is expected of them - call to action And finally - review, review, review!

When sending emails - it is important to consider regularly your email statistics, from open rates, click-through rates and conversion rates. Finding what is working and what is not working will help you develop a more targeted email marketing campaign, therefore increasing conversion rates.

## 1.5 Is Email Marketing Right for Your Business?

Here are the nine reasons you should critically consider using email marketing:

1. It Puts You In The Drivers Seat

As a professional Internet marketer, I can tell you it's a lot easier to get people to visit your website than it is to get them to come back. The majority of those visiting your site will not return unless you invite them back for a compelling reason to do so. Email marketing is how you invite them back to your site, and you can invite them whenever you want.

## 2. It's Easy To Get Started

Email marketing is easier today than at any other time in the history. Some wonderful services and tutorials can help you generate leads and stay in touch with your customers.

Not only that but if you decide that you don't have the time or don't want to learn how to do email marketing yourself, there are virtual assistants all over the world who are very capable of writing and sending your emails for you.

## 3. It's Affordable

There are three ways of going about email marketing.

1. You can do it yourself from your computer for free, but this is not a good idea for a lot of reasons. If you have more than 50 people on your list, you need something more professional.

2. You can hire the services of email marketers to host your list and help you run your campaign. This is a great solution starting at about $15/month for a list of up to 500 people, and they will take care of all the back-end technical issues.

3. The third solution is to purchase and install email marketing software on a dedicated server. Depending on the budget you have, the number of people on your list and your technical capabilities, one of these methods is going to work best for you.

4. It's Fast

Think how long it takes to type a letter, prepare an envelope, apply postage and have your message delivered. It takes days. And if you want to have it delivered next day, your only other option is to send it via FedEx or UPS or Express Mail with the Postal Service, and that's not cheap.

Email is instantaneous. It travels at the speed of light. So if you happen to have a marketing idea that comes to you in your sleep, you can roll out of bed and send it to your list before you wake up. Now that's fast, possibly dangerous, but fast.

## 5. It's Measurable

This is what I love most about email marketing. You can measure everything. You can determine who received your email, who opened your email, who acted on your offer, who passed your email on a friend and who opted out of your list. You can't do that with standard mail, and you can't do that with radio, TV or any other form of advertising.

## 6. It's Automated

Imagine spending an afternoon or a day creating an entire email marketing campaign and having it automatically start the moment your visitor signs up on your website. Now imagine this taking place 24/7 for as long as you're in business without ever having to look at it again.

Once you create your campaign, the software does the rest. You can automatically send everyone who signs up on your list a series of messages that move them closer to the sale while generating trust and branding yourself as the expert in your field.

## 7. It's Flexible

If you use TV, radio or print, you're limited in what you can do with that specific media. With email marketing, you can mix it up and keep your prospects interested.

## 8. It's Green

What kind of a conscientious human being would I be if I didn't mention that email marketing is good for the environment? It doesn't destroy the rain forest in Brazil or impact the living space of the Spotted Owl or Bald Eagle here in the United States.

Email marketing just does what it does best, with the full blessing of Al Gore and Ralph Nader. You can't get greener than that.

9. It's Effective

The most valuable thing email marketing does for you is it works. It positions you as the expert in your field; it builds credibility and trust, and it sells your products and services day in and day out.

# 1.6 Writing Emails That Are More Effective

Opt-in email marketing is a very popular and affordable marketing tool used by many different people who all have the same goal: to get their readers to take action of some kind. Writing emails that make people take action does not need to be complicated. There are a some simple tips you can follow to make your emails as effective (and profitable) as possible, such as testing different headlines and writing a clear call to action for your readers.

One tip that you can use to increase how effective your email marketing campaigns will be is to take advantage of any of the analytics and statistics that are provided by your email marketing program. There are a few key metrics that can give you some great insight into how effective your email marketing efforts truly are, such as the "open rate" and the "click-through rate." The open rate will tell you how many times the email was opened by your readers compared to the total number of emails sent out, and the click-through rate will tell you how many people clicked on any of the links in the email.

Obviously, if you want your email marketing campaign to be effective, then your readers need to at least click your email to open it and read it. Since the open rate is such an important number to focus on, you will want to do whatever you can to make it as high as possible. One of the most effective ways for maximizing how many times your email gets opened is to experiment with different headlines to see which one will get the highest response. The headline is the main thing that controls whether or not people will even click to open it, and once they open it now, you want them to take a certain action.

The next most important statistic is your click-through rate, and the best way to make this go as high as possible is to communicate effectively. Do not use a paragraph when a short sentence will do, and make sure that your call to action is very clear and compelling. Inform your reader what you would like them to do and tell them multiple times. Highlight the link that you want your readers to click on by putting it on a separate line, and list the link multiple times throughout the email. By focusing on these simple tips, you will be able to write emails that are more effective, and that receive a higher response.

## 1.7 Email Address List for email marketing

Online marketing though direct, is faceless as a service provider you are not in constant and direct contact with the end customers. This puts you in oblivion where you are not sure whether your product or service is liked by them or not. Email marketing is your way to reaching them and let the target audience know about your product and services. For this type of marketing, you need to procure Email Address List, which is up-to-date; cross checked and has the desired information.


For email addresses

There are many online companies which either sell or work on your behalf for email marketing. Later is a better option, as you do not have to worry as these companies can handle your Business Email Lists and do the needful.

For availing their service, you can either send them content for email or explain the requirement and let them prepare the details. However in the latter scenario, it is better to have a look at the draft and make sure it comes to you for approval. Certain companies have prepared different categories for the benefit of their clients. A sorted list gives a focused approach, and there is an assurance of an increase in revenue.

Few companies even have an option for specialty email lists. This comprises of Doctor Email List or Nurse Email List or Student Email List or Church Email List and others. These types of lists are beneficial for those who serve a niche market and do not have a big market for their product. By opting for such a list, you can expect to have a considerable return on investment.

## 1.8 Email Marketing Software and its Benefits

E-mail advertising and marketing software program are really practical - it might be utilized in practically all divisions of the business. However, a bulk e-mail application program does not call for an agreement-based e-mail advertising effort. This indicates that e-mail marketing software lessens the marketer's efforts as it distributes email advertisements based on the directory database with lists of subscribers who already gave their permission to obtain emails from advertising corporations.

So, how does the use of e-mail marketing software benefit your business?

Template creation

Whoever is accountable for the creation of templates, he is praised. At present, you won't have to struggle on how your email themes really should appear - from its colors, designs and graphics. Most e-mail advertising software contains a massive array of templates you'll be able to opt for from. Conversely, arriving at a specific template style doesn't put an end to your email. Email advertising and marketing software program ought to present a freedom for you to style your incredibly own stationery. If both do not satisfy you, some software program manufacturers offer you an in-house layout staff that could customize an e-mail template exclusively for your industry.

## Save time and operating charges

It doesn't matter how a lot of e-mail advertisements you might be about to send. It only needs a single bulk e-mail advertising and marketing operation to distribute them. Per se, excellent e-mail advertising, and marketing software possesses wonderful e-mail discharge rates. You wouldn't desire to waste a week just for those emails to be sent, would you?

Communicate consistently

Professionals say that subscribers are expected to be loyal in case you preserve a consistent communication with them. Do this by sending out emails concerning future promotions and markdowns. Your subscribers will keep coming back for extra and may even suggest your business to others.

Be specific - do not make unnecessary guesses

An advertising operation is useless should you will not have any idea if your clients receive your emails. For this, e-mail advertising software delivers the greatest benefit. Marketers might be able to track down their emails - if clients have read it or not and if they've subscribed to your newsletters or not. Knowing how your consumers react to your marketing and advertising technique is critical for you to strengthen your transactions and produce a brand new plan as to where your advertising business enterprise is heading.

Millions of men and women worldwide are already garnering the benefits that e-mail marketing software provider for their email advertising campaign. It's time that you do, too.

# Chapter 2: Social Media marketing and advertising

## 2.1 What Exactly Is Social Media?

Social media is basically a bunch of websites and online tools, that are used for interacting with others. Whether it is used to stay in touch with family overseas, or by businesses who want to reach out to their customers — social media is primarily about people communicating with other people.

Here is a list of the different types of social media that you can use:

•Social network websites: These are the types of websites that have been discussed briefly already, like Facebook and Twitter.

•Video and image networks: These are like regular social websites, but people use them to share images and videos. YouTube is a hugely popular website, where anyone can share their own videos, and possibly even become famous in the process.

•Blogs: Think of these as online journals, which are often written by ordinary people, although businesses are using them more and more.

•Podcasts: These are similar to radio shows, but they are streamed over the

Internet. They can be downloaded for later listening, making them great for busy people to enjoy.

•Social games: These days, many video games have online elements, or are played entirely over the Internet, with other people. Even the latest consoles and computer game systems usually have social media functions, where people can see what their friends have been playing, and share photos, images, and videos of their own gameplay. There are even social worlds that are similar to video games, but are purely for socializing with digital characters, in digital settings.

•Wikis: Have you ever visited Wikipedia? That is the most popular wiki, where users can publish, edit, and add to online, written content. They are like online encyclopedias, and can be about a vast range of topics.

As you can see, the Internet is gradually becoming one big social network, where the lines between traditional, and social, media are increasingly blurred. People are now connected in ways that were previously never thought possible, day and night, all the time.

## 2.2 Do You Need Social Media?

When you started reading this book, you might have been purely interested in learning a little about social media. However, you might be wondering if it's the right thing for you. Do you need to use social media in today's world? That is certainly a personal decision, but here are some reasons that you should use social media:

•People need people: Yes, you probably already have an active social network in your life, without needing to use a computer. In addition, everyone always likes to have at least some alone time, so they can just relax and unwind. People still need to be a part of a community, and it is part of human nature to want to be social. Social networks just make it a lot easier to do this.

•Growing your network: There has never been a better tool for expanding the network of people that you know. You might even find a new hobby that you never thought anyone in your area liked.

•Speaking your mind: It is easy to feel like just another number, especially in the modern world. Instead of feeling like the people who run the world are not listening, why not say what you think, by using social media? Unlike sending away letters to organizations, and then wondering if they were even read by anyone, you can interact and receive direct replies.

•Fighting isolation: If you find that you spend more time alone that you would like, social media can help. While people at first thought that the Internet would isolate people, it has been proven to do the opposite.

•Making real connections: You might use a digital device to access social media, but the connections that you will make with people are absolutely real.

That is certainly more social and "real" than watching television, or reading a newspaper, in your free time.

•Doing what matters: Thanks to social media, many people have realized that they are not alone in their beliefs and opinions. It is the ultimate way to interact with others who have similar points of view.

•Business: One of the newest areas of growth for business marketing is social media. If you operate your own company, it is the perfect place to reach out

and grab onto customers. Even for professionals who work with companies, there are plenty of new opportunities to find.

## 2.3 Blogs

## What Are Blogs?

"Blog" is a short form for "weblog." Blogs originally appeared as online diaries; however, today they have been transformed into full-fledged content management systems that many different types of sites can adapt to their users.

Some enormous sites use Wordpress and other blogging platforms that you would never suspect of employing free software. That provides evidence of the current popularity of blogging solutions.

There are many benefits connected with blogs, such as RSS feeds that can alert people and websites when there is an update on your blog.

Another great benefit is that you don't need any HTML, web design or programming knowledge to publish a website blog because the content management system makes it all easy for you.

To post a new article, all you have to do is log into your admin panel. Also, you can customize your site, manage plugins (software that adds various functions to your blog) and you can do a variety of other tasks.

Most people who are making money blogging are simply publishing articles, reviews, previews, ideas and advice on a topic that interests them.

Monetize a blog using affiliate links and banners, Adsense ads, by selling banner slots, by selling your product, and by a host of other methods. The different ways to earn money from a blog are endless.

Wordpress is  the most popular blogging software. This is simply a free script that you download from wordpress.org and then upload to your web host. Many web hosts have a one-click interface that lets you easily install Wordpress in seconds.

A great feature of Wordpress is the fact that readers can comment on your blog posts. This keeps all of your articles active in the search engines, generates increased interest and keeps people coming back to your site.

Blog comments are a good way to reach out to your readers -- do reply to the comments so that your readers know your care.

## Components of A Blog

If you've seen quite a few blogs, you may have a good idea of what it typically contains. Not all blogs are similar, so some blogs may have more things going on than others.

Here are the 5-basic elements of a blog:

1. Title- Located at the uppermost part of the article. The title is the one that initially captures the audience. It often has a picture or a message describing the article's title. Being the front line of your blog, you'd want to put something here that best describes your blog. The heading gives shows that the guest is on the right website. It's a static element in a website which can also double as a link back to the blog's homepage.


2. Blog Entries- The substance of an article is seen on blog entries. It's the heart of any article. A blog may continue to exist (sometimes) having only that. All the things that a blogger wants to convey go into blog posts which are posted from time to time. It's an ever-updating canvas of text, images, videos, and what-not. New blog posts are the things that readers look into. Since bloggers are famous for bringing the trend, it's a must to maintain or even surpass that expectation.

3. Navigation section- For visitors to get into the several pages of your blog, a navigation section is a must. Sidebar navigation is pretty common, but some bloggers get creative and put the navigation links elsewhere, like just below the header or at the bottom of the page. It would be a lot easy to find archived blog posts or sort out articles using navigational links.

4. About me- This page is intended for the writer. A post about the blog's history and writer's life story is set up in the "MySpace" page. It should not necessarily be an autobiography; just a few sentences would suffice. Other bloggers do it using a question and answer style while some still opt to use the conventional method which is essay writing. Contact information may also be added to this page so that readers, including advertisers, can reach you.

5. Feedback - A blog is fascinating if each opinion can be heard. The typical interaction field of a blogger and a reader happens in the remarks section of a blog site.

Ideas are exchanged and developed through digital discourse. A blogger can also enjoy soaking up on pride as readers leave footprints of praises about his articles. Famous articles are frequent topics everywhere.

## Steps To Develop Your Blog

Well, you've thought why your blog ranked low over at search engines, and this has been quite some time now. So what's the main problem here? Although nothing disastrous can happen, it's also not a good idea to stay on the safe side. Remember, blogs are updated every day, and that's why you also need to be in line with the competition. As online competition moves on, latest updates and inventive blog methods are implemented to provide better blogs.Blog upgrades are indeed vital to make your blogs updated.

Consequently, to improve a blog, it doesn't need "full repair". You can simply add, remove or edit little components of your blog to make it better. Here are some things you can start with:

1. Incorporate social network to your blog - Internet users spend more time in their social network than in any other website. It just follows that your blog should also have its social network profile. Provide social network links in your blog profile to let simply visitors click "add" or "follow" your page. An even better the idea is to add a social network feed widget. This will then let your readers get instant messages (using these feed widgets) in obtaining the latest blog posts you've created.

2. Do a template "face-lift "- Online readers always want to have the most recent website look, and you might wish to consider this on your blog's front page. It may not be up to the latest standard anymore, regarding color and design. Just upgrade your front page using the best templates, background color, and readable fonts. After that, you can move on to deeper aspects of your blog like adding a favicon and tweaking its CSS code.

3. Restructure your blog - Blog site features that are considered obsolete can be fixed once you reorganize it.

To make your blog organized, just add the most recent blog categories implemented online.

4. Implement the latest techniques - Blogging is not just about publishing the text. Implementing other methods besides blog articles is yet another way to impart your message to people. How about posting a video now and then? The addition of infographics to your blog is a great idea. Implementing more methods for your blog will surely enhance traffic. If your niche really can't be converted into a video or infographic, try to rearrange your blog entry such that it is presented in a magazine-like fashion.

5. Enhance your writing skills - To improve writing further this skill, you have to harness it continuously by practicing and learning from other experts in writing. In writing blog articles, you should not apply the ideas that are limited to you only. Make an effort to discover new words and use the storytelling techniques you learned from school.

These things can make an enormous difference on your blog.

Indeed, there is no such thing a perfect blog article since it will depend on the readers 'point of view' in your blog. Remember, if your blog is not up to date, there's a chance you might end up losing a lot of your online readers.

## Free Blog Marketing Tips

You've probably come across numerous blog marketing tips on the net these days, yet often find yourself searching for more as most of these helpful hints, claiming they are exceptional, are all but a bunch of senseless and pointless guidelines. Given this state of affairs, most blogs toil in anonymity with a hope that sooner or later, their biggest and grandest break will come to pass.

It is every blogger's dream to own a blog that will stand out in the vast virtual world. Hence, as one way of fueling your blog, here are blog marketing tips that would mainly improve the popularity of your niche and drive more visitors to your virtual little island.

1. Blog Content: Do you often wonder the common denominator of most popular blogs on the net these days? For one, it's their being controversial. These blogs are never afraid of writing contents that would oppose to common norms. Owners of these blogs have their voices and write contents that would be of great interest to the vast readership. Another thing is the ability of a blog to offer readers useful information and solution to frequently asked queries. Readers would go for a blog that provides practical and constructive answers to major inquiries. If you're able to convey these to your online readers and visitors, you'll inevitably land on top ranking pages in major search engines.


2. Blog Frequency: Updating your blog on a regular basis leads to blog popularity. Posting contents at a minimum of 3-5 times in a week is more than enough to fuel your

blog. Bloggers frequently bringing up to date information on their blogs have high probabilities of being included in various search engines' news index and has excellent chances of getting into top search results pages. So, if you want your blog to stand out and be noticed by prospective clienteles, always provide an updated and interesting topic on a regular footing.

3. Blog Distribution: This is considered as one of the most salient blog marketing guidelines that bloggers should pay particular attention to. If you are to market your blog, RSS/Atom feed can be endorsed for better blog exposure within the blogosphere. This offers greater advantages weigh against regular sites without RSS feeds. This type of blog distribution paves the way for marketing and promoting your blog not just on major search engines but also on major RSS search engines with the likes of Feedster, Google Blog Search, and Bloglines among others.

4. Blog with Keywords: This is an additional blog optimization that facilitates in fueling one's blog. If you want to get your blog to appropriate landing pages on major search engines, you can use popular keywords and keyword phrases relevant to your post. You can also make use of blog software template as a way of making your blog titles in text links, in Meta description tag, and in the title tag.

5. Blogs must be bound in and out Link to your blog to various online directories particularly to blog/RSS-specific directories for better optimization. Conversely, you can thematically link out to highly trafficked websites and blogs for better search engine visibility and identity on the web.

So, who says your blog should toil in obscurity? With the blog mentioned above marketing tips, you'll obtain a good grasp of improved brand reputation, credibility, better client relations and increased profits and sales in no time.

## 2.4 Facebook

## What is Facebook?

It's the only one of the best online tools for small business to come along in the last decade. Facebook can help you reach new customers engage your loyal fans and drive sales to your site.

Facebook isn't just about getting likes- it's about keeping them.

While the debate about the value of a like or a fan has gone up and down over the years, one thing is clear: The more users interact with your fan page, the more you'll show up in their friends' news feeds. But Facebook interaction doesn't happen in a vacuum. You need to get the conversation started.

Share new products, exciting news and stories about your business on your Facebook page. Just as people love to see behind the scenes of their favorite TV show, your

Facebook fans want to see more of your business. Share photos of your workshop, videos from trade shows and any other media you think your fans will enjoy getting them talking.

## What makes Facebook an important marketing platform?

Facebook can give you the marketing platform which you always wanted. Find out what makes Facebook an important marketing platform. One of the reasons is the branding opportunity of Facebook. It is a recommended practice for the businesses to secure their brand name through available domain names.

In a similar manner, they are advised to obtain their brands through Facebook and other media sites. On making a profile on Facebook, it assigns a unique URL to it for quickly accessing it afterward. Using your brand name in the URL would help you in its marketing. You would also be protecting your brand name from possible misrepresentations from the competitors' side.

Business websites benefit a lot if they have good content on them as well as good SEO is practiced on it besides having some good links. Content and SEO are specifically done on the website, but good links can be obtained through various ways. Link building is done in two ways - naturally or by paying. Getting links naturally are far better than paying for them.

Facebook allows you to obtain links naturally. Facebook lets linking back to your website through your profile. Using links pointing to your website is allowed on Facebook. If you want to use anchor texts, you can do that easily. The links on your Facebook profile would be referred to as the inbound links to your website. You can post company news besides promoting your business.

Getting some extra traffic is no issue through Facebook. Using social media sites is on the rise these days, so marketers should develop marketing strategies targeting these sites. For marketing, you need to contact lots of people and through Facebook you can access many people so why not use Facebook as your marketing platform? Networking opportunities on Facebook lets you carry out your marketing practices on a wide scale. If there are no networks, you won't be able to operate your business productively.

## 2.5 LinkedIn

# What is LinkedIn?

When it comes to online networking, Facebook and Twitter are the names you'll hear most often. LinkedIn can help small business owners like you develop your brand, business, and connections in just a few minutes per day. Read on to learn what is LinkedIn and how it will help you find commercial success.

LinkedIn's 175 million members did 4.2 billion professional searches in 2011. Did they find you?

Many business owners overlook LinkedIn, believing it's a network searching jobs and potential employees. You can use the site to build up your network, online and off, and keep your business top of mind for long-term customers, potential customers, and suppliers

# Tips on getting started

To build your personal profile just follow the form. Fill each box with the requested information, like current and past work history, and upload a current photo.

Next, search for contacts. If you have a Gmail account, you can use your Gmail address book to make the search faster. Adding a personal message to remind each contact how they know you.

Once you've made some connections, request recommendations from those you've worked with. This helps to build your credibility and tells more of your story than your work history alone. As you make new connections offline, add them to your LinkedIn network.

Now it's time to build your business page:

A business page shows customers, suppliers, and vendors that you're interested in the success of your business.

Your business page will display your logo, a brief description of your business and your business's connections. Businesses can follow each other to stay up-to-date on each other's latest news and developments, and like on Facebook, businesses can also have fans.

Learning what is LinkedIn and building your profile is just the beginning. Read on for ways leverage your networks to build your business

Find new vendors: Search LinkedIn for vendors you'd like to work with to learn more about their businesses. If you have a standard connection, ask for an introduction through E-Mail.

Find new suppliers: On LinkedIn, you can learn a lot about companies you're interested in working with. See what other companies they do business with, read recommendations and even connect with their customers to ask for a review.

Build your reputation: There's a LinkedIn group for every interest and industry. Join several active (meaning people are posting in them regularly) groups and participate in the conversation. Look for questions you can answer and interesting links you can share to build your reputation as an expert in your field.

Check out the competition: Discover which stores and suppliers are your competitors working with? This may sound covert, but it's not spying - it's keeping an eye on your industry so you can make informed choices about your business.

Now you know what is LinkedIn you can discover new ways to leverage it for your business. I'd love to hear about your LinkedIn experiences!

## LinkedIn Marketing

LinkedIn marketing isn't just for job seekers or Fortune 500 CEOs anymore. Today more small business owners are taking advantage of the business networking platform to find new customers and build their brand.

Steps to get you started:

Begin with your personal LinkedIn profile

Instead of merely listing your experience, use your LinkedIn profile to tell the story of your professional life. Include phrases that highlight your brand's message and build up list contacts that know you and have done business with you. When it comes to connections, quality beats quantity. Ask your contacts to write recommendations that describe why they choose you. Next, move on to your company profile.

Make your company profile your brand's digital home base

Anyone can build a website and advertise their brand, but a LinkedIn marketing company profile gives you credibility. Ensure you use the same company name in the current employment section of your personal profile and your business profile to link the two. For example, if you company name is Creative Wares LLC, ensure you use the LLC on both.

Place your logo to be your profile photo and fill in all of the available boxes to build a solid profile, including founding date, company size, and industry. Craft a message that accurately describes your business, your goals and what you have to offer your customers.

Utilize the products and services tabs for LinkedIn Marketing

This is the best part of your company page. It allows you introduce your products to new customers and offer a place for existing customers to recommend your products to their contacts. Don't forget to link each product to its page on your website so users who want to buy or learn more can do so easily.

Invite your contacts and customers to follow you

Invite your LinkedIn personal contacts who have worked with your business to follow your company, and add a LinkedIn follow button to your company website and email signature.

Update your company status, weekly

Status updates help you to get on the radar of new clients. Post status updates on upcoming events, company news, sales or any other information that will grab your followers.

Now that you are LinkedIn marketing you can take full advantage! Join groups to share your expertise, post ads to drum up new business and learn as much as you can about the world's largest business network.

## 2.6 Twitter

# What is Twitter and Twitter Marketing?

Twitter marketing is a simple, an effective way to keep in touch with your customers is to find new ones and build up a following for your brand.

While there are plenty of long lists online covering what to do/not to do on Twitter, they are often loaded with opposing recommendations. You can learn the basics and get started today by following my 4 Twitter marketing tips for beginners:

Share don't spray

Resist the urge to tweet only company related news and sales. Introduce yourself, learn how your followers respond to different types of posts and tailor what you share to their interests. Use a free analytics program like

Hootsuite to discover which tweets earn the most clicks, retweets, and responses.

Advance search is your friend

Type your search term in Twitter's main search box to use it. Once the search results in load, click the cog button in the right-hand corner of the search results box to select advanced search.

Here you can search your company name or product name to keep up on what's being said about your brand. Search for your keywords to find people looking for products like yours, or asking questions in your niche. Strive to help rather than to sell. Those looking to buy will be more likely to come to you after you've extended a helping hand.

Change your headlines to share a blog post more times

Twitter followers tend to opt out if you constantly send the same tweet six times per day. You can still share your new blog post a few times by changing the headline tweet you use to share it. Stay on topic, but offer a different angle in each tweet to intrigue readers who skipped the first one.

Automate to save time on Twitter marketing

While it's frowned upon to automate all of your tweets, web apps like Hoot suite can help save you social media minutes. Schedule tweets to remind your customers of upcoming deals or new items at peak hours when you're too busy to tweet live.

Use hashtags wisely

Hashtags, or the use of a number sign before a word, help users searching for specific topics find your posts. For example, if you're tweeting about your newest handmade jewelry designs, adding #handmade to the end of your tweet will ensure it shows up in a search. This handy tool is best used sparingly, so don't overload your tweets by adding a # to every word. At most use two per tweet and use a site like hashtags.org to find out what keywords are trending in your niche.

Do you still have questions about Twitter marketing? Or have a tip of your own to share? Please post them in the comments.

## Tips to Using Twitter

If you have asked your friends and family if they are on Twitter, they may or may not know what you are talking about. While everyone and their mother seem to know about MySpace and Facebook, many people appear to be finally learning what Twitter is. The thing is, though, Twitter, while some compare it to the other social network sites, is more geared towards professional adults than anything else. While some young people may sign up for an account, they do not last long on there.

This is probably because you cannot post pretty graphics, write blogs that are ten pages long, and stalk the lives of other people through the millions of pictures they are posting of themselves. With all of that taken into consideration, Twitter is the place to be for the working adult that is professional and looking to expand their business through connection and customer relations. There are in fact seven popular ways people use Twitter.

1. Expand Your Circle Of Friends

With the help of Twitter, one can   follow people who are of like mind. Those who are in the same field as you or who have the same interests are often the people that you will find yourself following. These people will follow your Twitter account as well since you all have so much in common. The people you follow on Twitter may never come to be anything more than an Internet friendship, but that does not mean that it is not a friendship that has its place and its value in your life.

2. Learn About Those You Admire

Whether you are following an actor, a singer, or your favorite business person, you can follow their account. Their comments may give you an insight into who they are and how they run a business. You may also learn a few tips and tricks from the people you admire without even realizing it. By making some connection with the people, you admire you can see what it is that you want to be.

## 3. Keep Your Family Informed

If your mother wants to know every time your new baby does something cute or special, you may find that you are tired of placing twenty phone calls a day. However, there is need to ensure that your relatives are not missing out on the important or special things that are taking place throughout your day or week. By placing easy to type messages or comments on Twitter, your family can see everything that is happening and feel as though they are being kept in the loop.

## 4. Become Famous In Your Right

Many people find that they need a fast, efficient, and cheap way to advertise themselves. Maybe you are starting a new local play, or an article you wrote just became published in a magazine. By placing a simple and sweet comment on your Twitter page, those following you will know about your recent accomplishments and will want to check them out.

## 5. Learn How To Open Up

Those that find they have a hard time opening up to people, even with the simplest thing, find that Twitter helps them overcome those obstacles. By placing a comment or two a day you can open up to those following you and see the wonderful responses that come from such an act.

## 6. Teach Others About Your Work Or Faith

When you reach out to others, there is something wonderful being felt by those who have been taught and those doing the teaching. Many people find that they can touch the lives of many by simply posting a comment or two each day about something inspirational.

## 7. Generate Traffic And Make Money

Though you may not be selling directly from the Twitter site, you can make use of it as a way to bring in more people. You can generate more traffic to a site of yours, gain more associates, and most importantly make more money. You will see that with enough dedication you will be able to earn a good bit of money by using the tools available to you, such as Twitter.

## 2.7 Instagram

## What is Instagram

Instagram is a social media site that gives people the freedom to take a picture or any image, apply digital filters and share on social media platform. The images that are taken appear like the Polaroid or Kodiak Instamatic film (square,) rather than the typical digital picture size.

## Ways of gaining Instagram Followers

Why is it useful for your business?

1. Make Personality:

Instagram permits you to make an identity for your business. You can take photos of your workspace, of occasion's occurrence in the workplace, deals you are having, a new stock that recently arrived, or even the outside perspective. Whatever you favor. Simply ensure it gives viewers an inside look at what your business is about and who is in the business.

2. Improve trust level:

It improves the trust relationship, particularly in an online world. As we advance into the world where more of communications are based online, individuals are looking for individual to individual contact. By demonstrating your grinning face as a photo, your client knows you are a genuine business with live bodies behind it. On the off chance that you invest a considerable measure of energy in the telephone, this is additionally a decent approach to get some publicity in.

3. Make Community:

Instagram permits you to make a group around pictures and your items. I have specified this in a past post, and I'll say it again here. Instagram is a flourishing group additionally an open group. Individuals are sharing things from spots to items and everything in the middle. It is not unprecedented for another individual to remark on a photograph of yours. You may considerably think about how they discovered you. Grasp it! This is the thing that this group is about and damnation, it is ideal! Instagram marketing software is useful for creating some the account at a time, along with it, we can also manage different Instagram account easily by using the automation feature supported by this software application.

The most efficient methods to pick up a huge Instagram followers is:

1. Begin snapping-

The primary principle of any social organization is to start doing it! That is regularly the hardest deterrent. I would prefer not to hear that you're a terrible picture taker either. Nobody is an awful picture taker.

## 2. Let people find you by using hashtags-

Hashtags are the manner by which individuals easily search you so never try to ignore the power of hashtags, always try to include them in your picture description part. You can use Instagram marketing software to search for some of the common popular hashtags which have the higher rate of use. I had explored different avenues regarding this and saw my photos got more likes when I included these hashtags. Use hashtags that incorporate your image or item name, additionally hashtags that are pertinent to your industry.

## 3. Try to search for your item or business-

This proves to be useful to a nearby business. When you discover your business or brand make a point to like the photograph and leave a remark. When you locate your careful area ensure you remark on those photographs and welcome them back.

4. Availability-

Join your photographs to an area when it bodes well. You don't need to do this unfailingly, yet you should do it if you have a nearby business.

5. Social Promotion-

Advance your Instagram page on your site, in your shop, and on your online networking channels. Share your photographs when you post them on Twitter and your Facebook business page. This is a simple one. No reasons.

# 2.8 Social Media Marketing Tools for Your Business

Internet marketing should span many different social media channels to be able to capture as many potential leads as feasible. But it can often be difficult to remain on top of social media campaigns, especially if you have some platforms to maintain. With social media promoting software, you can keep track of all your social media business profiles and activity in one effortless place. Whether or not you use Facebook, Twitter, YouTube, or perhaps a combination of other social media sites to interact with customers, the subsequent social media promoting tools will help you monitor each channel and integrate them with your email activities, e-commerce software, and internet site.

Convert Social:

With many tools to use, including a social media scheduling tool, Convert Social is designed to make it easier to market your marketing and advertising communications via multiple social media channels. You can post your promoting content from RSS feeds and even schedule future marketing campaigns. By monitoring all your stations in one place, you are more probably to spot relevant conversations and successfully engage with your target audience.

Dire Message Labs:

With Direct Message Labs, you can rapidly find excellent social media platforms for your particular business, depending on your target viewers and other crucial aspects. In addition to assisting you to create new profiles for the best suited social media sites the software allows your marketing and advertising team to build new posts and submit various media content material across many platforms from one hassle-free location.

HootSuite:

Taking care of multiple social media stations and monitoring the overall performance of each one is made easier with the HootSuite dashboard. You can schedule social media communications, determine where and when your company is mentioned online, and measure the traffic of each social media site. As an item of analytics software, it can be invaluable for any advertising team, providing multiple article scenarios that can be shared with your colleagues or consumers.

Kwanzoo:

The promoting activities from Kwanzoo can run on your web page, inside e-mail newsletters, on social media sites and affiliate web pages, and on paid advertising channels. By running researchers and other interactive events combined with users into customers. Users can also share offers, assisting in spreading the word concerning your business. And since the software is completely cloud-based, there's no need to set up any software on your computers. With analytics software included, you will also find out how good your activities are performing.

Loop Lingo:

This promoting tool is advantageous if you need to boost your social media following and appeal to more potential customers. By presenting special offers and discounts at the point of sale, it gives your clients a motivation to make prompt purchases and add your company to their social networks. You pay Loop Lingo in the event it generates a sale, and with analytics software to track your marketing successes and failures, it's worth considering.

Posting:

This useful social media device enables you to schedule posts to different online social media platforms, monitor conversations about your brand, and reply to feedback, all from one handy area. It's just like a social media inbox for your own small business. You may also receive notifications whenever a keyword or key phrase seems on selected social media sites (for illustration, the name of your company).

Sensible:

Much like other social media monitoring platforms, Sendible also helps you keep track of all your social media profiles in one location, making it less complicated to interact with customers and keep track of overall brand performance. Simultaneously updating quite a few media channels at once can be extremely helpful, especially in case you lack the time or resources. Sensible helps you accomplish this with its extremely versatile software, keeping you up to date with your target audience via social media, e-mail, or SMS.

As social media marketing and advertising become even more prevalent, it is essential harnessing the power of some of these promoting tools. When you know how much you have to spend on social media marketing and advertising, why not consider using one or more of these types of tools to make your promoting strategies more effective and cost-efficient?

## 2.9 Social Media Promotion Don'ts

There are countless social media marketing experts, who are having to rehash their strategies to promote services, products or campaigns through social media. Unfortunately, the "don'ts" of social media promotion are often forgotten in the midst of all the hype about the power of promotion through this medium. Some businesses end up using approaches that can be counterproductive, to say the least. You should avoid such pushy, tactless approaches to promote your blog or website, or services or products you offer.

Social media marketing without a strategy

Every event, non-profit organization and company need a well thought-out promotional plan. Start with a clear-cut campaign approach that will be sure to bring in tangible results. Create a clear and comprehensive social media advertising plan that lists the things you will use to target your market segment. Put in a diligent effort to implement the campaigns and monitor their success using an efficient reporting system. If you do not have a specific, unambiguous plan tailored to your needs, you will not get the results you want and end up annoying a lot of people with unwelcome, push promotions.

Suggesting all your friends and acquaintances to buy your product

If you are promoting your product on social networking sites like Twitter and Facebook, don't force your online connections to buy the product. A subtle suggestion or mentioning the product's best features is fine, but hard-selling it to acquaintances is a strict no-no.

Posting purely public comments and links on others' walls

Posting purely promotional comments are misguided attempts at marketing and will only result in irritating other people, both the owner of the wall as well as visitors. Worse, you could end up on their black lists, or you could be reported as a spammer.

Sticking to your followers and friends lists alone for advertising

Badgering followers and friends are downright annoying - and cannot, by any stretch of the imagination, be considered marketing. It is not an approach that will get you very far regarding visibility and market reach. If you want a significant web presence, you will have to look beyond your small circle of social media followers and friends.

## Responding to every comment or feedback that is negative

It may be tempting to reply to every comment you receive, positive or negative, but you should understand that along with supporters, you will also find your share of detractors. Do not act on impulse and post extremely opinionated replies or comments. Share opinions on comments posted by visitors and encourage participation. Involvement with customers and visitors is essential to winning their trust and also understand how they react to your product. It is important that you pay attention to what your customers have to say about your product. Listen to their complaints regarding your product and offer suitable solutions or explanations.

Social media marketing certainly requires good manners online and can flourish with a well thought-out strategy. Treat the online audience with respect and consideration just as you would treat your best customers.

# Chapter 3: Affiliate marketing

## 3.1 What Is Affiliate Marketing and How Does It Work For Me?

Simply put, affiliate marketing is the process by which a company rewards an individual (the affiliate) for the marketing efforts of that affiliate. The reward for this marketing effort is normally based on a sale, but it could be based on another specified action that the company defines in its affiliate program. Depending on the program it may be based how many times the company's ad is viewed on the affiliate's website, or how many times that ad is clicked on. Whatever the exact program, the affiliate is selling other people's products instead of his products. This is the short answer to the first half of the question-"What is affiliate marketing and how does it work for me?"

As an affiliate, the company will provide you with your unique link to their website, or some other specified site, from which a person might make a purchase. Any person clicking through that link is identified as a person that did so as a result of your efforts, and thus you get credit for any purchase that occurs. This typically rewards you with a specified dollar amount or a specified percentage of that sale.

As an affiliate marketer, you have the freedom to market the company's product any way you choose within the guidelines of the company's program. This means that you can set up a standard e-commerce website as a base to market the products, or you might set up a blog site, or run an email campaign. Indeed, you might do all of the above or even implement any number of other marketing strategies. The point is that you need to develop a marketing strategy to be effective.

There are two critical issues when developing a strategy, and answering the second part of the question- "What is affiliate marketing and how does it work for me?" How do get people to click on your affiliate link, and what happens when they do click through.

Having a constant traffic flow to your affiliate link is a necessary component to your success. If people don't see your link they certainly can't click on it. The creation of a blog site is a good place to start. It is relatively painless to set up and can even be done for free using WordPress. Writing interesting posts that contain contextual links or using banner ads are two proven ways to generate clicks. The buildup of the popularity of your blog site, however, generally will take time.

Another way to generate traffic is through article writing. Assuming you can produce an article that is at least somewhat interesting you can then use someone else's website to help get traffic to your site.

Having a professional sales team on the other end of your affiliate link that will treat your prospect in a truly professional manner is the second critical issue that is vital to your business. This may be the sales force for the company itself, or it may be outside agency acting for the company on your behalf. This allows you the freedom to be creative without having actually to close the sale. Partnering with an enterprise that conducts its business the way you want to conduct business is truly the only way to go.

There is more that can be discussed concerning the question-What is affiliate marketing and how does it work for me? But this much is certain, learning how to create a consistent traffic flow and having a professional sales partner is vital.

If you are seriously looking for legitimate, proven methods to generate multiple streams of income online, then click read on and discover how affiliate marketing can work for you too.

## 3.2 Affiliate Marketing Tips - How to Find a Niche Market

Knowing how to find a niche market is an important skill that all affiliate marketers should learn. The more you practice this process, the better you will become, eventually, it will be like second nature. Niche hunting should be an enjoyable process and one that you can do anywhere. Below are five places you can start your search.

1. Something you love:

One thing that sells better than anything else is passion. If you have a passion for the niche, you are promoting then this will show in the copy that you write. It is infectious, and will translate into sales. If you choose a niche in an area or market that you love you are halfway there.

If you spend your free time fishing with a great fishing rod, choose this as your product to promote. You will be doing a lot of writing, and you will find it easier to complete this task if you love what you are writing about.

2. Products that you use:

If you have recently found a product that solved a problem for you, you can bet others have the same problem too. You have a ready-made campaign right in front of you. Choosing a product you know about because you use it will give you a great advantage. When you write, this first-hand knowledge will show through, and make the process run a lot more smoothly.

3. Amazon or eBay:

If you are still stuck for ideas ready-made niches in profitable areas are online just waiting for you. Both Amazon and eBay have affiliate programs you can join, plus they both have special areas of their website that will give you information on what people want, and what they are buying. Amazon's is called Amazon bestsellers, and eBay has the eBay pulse. Both these sites are worth a visit, and the information they give is pure gold if you are stuck for a direction to go in.

4. Question sites:

There are a variety of sites where people can ask questions or sites that tell people how to do something. These kinds of places are a niche hunters paradise. Look for what people are asking or popular "how to" articles, and give answers in the form of products

5. Events or Holidays:

Seasonal events are niches in themselves. Each will bring specific needs that you can fulfill. Many online marketers make a whole business just exploiting these short specialized periods. Just as many shy away from them because of their seasonality, as they prefer year-round evergreen sectors. This leaves certain areas of these seasonal events easy targets for sales.

These are by no means the only methods you can use. If you are out to learn how to find a niche market, use your imagination. Profitable niches can be found in the most unlikely places. Have fun and happy hunting.

I love finding new niches and keywords that I can use to build my business. .

## 3.3 Drawing Quality Targeted Users to Your Website, Fast!

Everyone desires their Website to have high traffic. The Internet has become a powerful medium for communicating with customers, increasing sales and developing brand recognition. Knowledge has become collective, with Wikipedia having 100 million hours of human thought invested in it. The competition is stiffening each day, and the Internet users are becoming highly selective and impatient. Therefore, if your site isn't easy to navigate or doesn't have the certain finesse to set it apart from the billions of others, users will quickly abandon your site and take their business elsewhere. So, what does it take to garner high traffic website growth and to maintain it?

There are many things you can do to cause traffic growth each month. Each approach demands its specific resources. In this book, we list down some key, non-technical tips that we believe can help business owners to increase their Website traffic proactively.

## 3.4 Tips to create High Traffic Website Growth

1. Value Proposition

Identify your site's value proposition. Remember, your site is there for a purpose. There must be a reason people surf your site or buy something from you instead of your competitors. What is your site's value to your visitors? You must be very clear on your value proposition. If you have nothing valuable to your visitors, then you have no need for a high traffic site. And if you have no need for it, you probably will not get it no manner how hard you try. Once you identified your value proposition, build your site around your value proposition. It is crucial to present your value proposition in a manner that is very clear to your visitors, especially for visitors visiting your site for the first time.

2. Quality Content

Content is king! Focus on your value proposition. Have lots of quality content that revolve around your site's value. Enforce and not dilute your value proposition. Focus on writing what the visitors are interested in, describe the benefits (not features) of the product, explain how to use the product, provide articles about the industry, stories about customers, projections, reviews, etc. In gist, focus on providing genuine, quality value content and let the word of mouth do the rest. Do not let quantity precedes over quality. Quantity without quality is easier to produce, but the Internet already contains more quantity than any one of us can absorb in our lifetime.

3. Tapping into existing Social Network

Tap into existing social network such as Facebook, Twitter or mySpace to harness the marketing power of social networking. Connect with people on the social networks. Inform them about your Website's business. This may peak the interest of someone in your network, and you may have just gained a prospective sale without much effort and cost. You can also post a link or a video clip to tell your followers or whoever that views your posts, how excited you are about the launch of your Website and invite them to check it out. Many will disregard your message, but those that don't are your prospective customers. Remember, it's called social networking because it group like-minded people together. And since you are a member of that group, this group of people will probably be interested in your services and may help you out. Activate the millions out there!

4. Search Engine Optimization

A good rule of thumb for the Internet is if you want to know about something or purchase something, there's probably already a Web site just for that. The catch is finding it. However, many companies still approach Search Engine

Optimization, Online / Offline Marketing, and Web Analytics as an afterthought. They view these marketing strategies as a sequential activity after the development of a website, or worse, as a fallback plan when the site is not having enough traffic. Planning of the e-commerce site and SEO/SEM/Web analytics are often disconnected. This is a serious mistake. We highly recommend that you cater for SEO right at the beginning. By incorporating SEO guidelines into your site design, you will avoid the headache of having to get back and revamp your low-traffic site. Importantly, the proper implementation of SEO strategies is not only to get you ranked high in search engines, but it is also a way for you to create a better user experience for your visitors. Proper implementation of SEO strategies will get you targeted traffic, not just traffic; that is, only visitors interested in your site will check your site out. This translates to happy visitors who could get what they want and ultimately return to your site again. In fact, for established

Website, repeat visits from the main underlying reason for continual long-term traffic growth.

## 3.5 How To Get High-Quality Backlinks

We know that backlinks are advantageous for your website, particularly for SEO purposes. However, many people fail to recognize the importance of getting quality backlinks, thus, instead of helping their site rank better and get the better-targeted traffic they're hurting their website by linking to poor and irrelevant websites.

So how do you get high-quality backlinks?

Through Press Release

Get quality backlinks from places that matter for your site by writing Press Release (PR) for news and press websites. If your PR is well-written, then there's a good chance that authority sites and news sites will pick it up and use if for their sites.

Submitting your PRs to every news site you know can be very demanding and hectic. Thus, you should know how to use distribution services to help you distribute your content to proper channels. PRWeb is what most SEO experts recommend.

Through Social Bookmarking

Getting backlinks from high-ranking sites, such as sites loved by search engines like social bookmarking sites will pump up your SEO and Page Rank. Social bookmarking sites allow people to "bookmark" their favorite pages to read later, and this can be a great avenue for you to start getting targeted traffic and free backlinks. It's almost hitting two birds with one stone.

Trough Reviews and Testimonials

Writing honest and unbiased testimonials for products and services you've used in the past is a good way to establish your name and brand online as a reputable business. If you display your reviews on your website, and people search for its keyword in search engines, your page will show up on the results page.

Make sure you write good, unbiased, informative, and comprehensive reviews that people can use.

## Through Article Submission

Article submission is often criticized for its efficacy. The truth of the matter is, it works, as a matter of fact, it's widely considered as the best SEO strategy to rank the website for its primary keyword. Search engines love article directory sites, especially Google, where its SEO puts a huge emphasis on valuable and helpful content. However, this strategy is pretty demanding, and it only works to those who are diligent in writing much good quality and highly valuable articles to the right article directory sites.

You need to keep submitting quality and valuable articles to article submission sites until you hit the number one spot and continue submitting to remain on top.

These are just 4 of the many things you can do to get high-quality backlinks. You can always use all these methods or focus your efforts on one or two, depending on your skills, time, and resources.

If you want real income at the comforts of your home without having to take orders from anyone, nothing beats the opportunities you find with online marketing business.

# Chapter 4: Brand Building Strategy

Brand building is not only communicating and exposing your brand but also a process of creating value to the customers. This entirely covers all the things that the customers know, feel and experience about the business in totality.

There are three types of brand namely service brand, retail brand, and product. The service brand is built on culture knowledge and experience. Retail brand is developed as a mixture of products and service. Finally, the product brand is built on the experience of their product.

Based on the above three types of brands you can decide on brand building strategy. First of all, you need to define your brand and state what it stands for. You need to tell about its effects and also why your brand is important for. Then you need to develop some differentiation to attract attention to be outstanding amongst the competitors. As you come up with a unique value for the brand, then you need to use a good brand strategy to position your brand in such a way that the consumers will be able to see your brand and appreciate them. If you need your brand to get appreciation and gain success, you should have to personalize it by giving your brand an identity.

Once your brand gets an identity, the consumer tries to experience the personality of your brand on the whole. This brand then goes through the range of motions. It depends on the brand building strategy, whether your brand grows in strength or be in the dormant state. It is essential to know clearly about your brand strategy and how you will implement it. You need to adopt the strategies that will add value to your consumers and also help them develop the right views of your company and what it truly stands for. You should try to know your customers need properly.

Product branding strategies help to establish a product within the market and to build a brand that will grow in a saturated marketplace. The product is a broad category that ranges from physical goods, tourism to handling the celebrities. People just don't buy a product; they wait for the product which meets their requirements, and they go for it. Anything which the company produces to satisfy the consumer's needs and demands is known as a product. Increasing a brand's relevance to a broader consumer segment requires a clear perception should be ahead of customers need and dreams.

The 4 P's that the company forms a strategy are product, place, price and promotion. One of the important aspects of product strategy is branding. Branding means a process of developing an identity for the product to create a sort of impression in the customer's mind. To build this identity involves designing the logo of the product and developing a strategy to create a point of difference from their competitors. Hence, the brand which reaches the high level of awareness enjoys the customer's loyalty thereby developing brand equity. The packaging of the products also forms part of product branding strategy.

The success of the company lies, on creating a unique product identity and branding strategy. Everything depends on the customer's decision to purchase will be based on the product and branding strategy.

# Conclusion

As a small business owner, keeping up with the competition can be extremely challenging. The race to get the next dollar from your customer base sometimes requires squeezing your prices so low that the margins are barely keeping your doors open.

While looking at your business sales results have you noticed that sales are stagnating or decreasing? Are you beating your head against the wall considering your available options to increase the traffic coming into your business thereby increasing your sales? If all of the solutions that you are coming up with are 20th-century solutions, you are actually losing the battle of business survival.

Media like television, radio and print are costly and slow in growing business in the "right now" the 21st century.

Everyone knows that television is great in establishing name recognition when advertising is repetitive enough to become accepted in the minds of its' viewers. The problem with television is that it is extremely expensive to create, produce and put on the air.

Radio on the other hand is less expensive than television but again too expensive for most small businesses to maintain over an extended period of time. Additionally, radio is not nearly as effective in building name recognition because consumers are not listening to radio as much in the 21st century.

Finally, there is the great-grandfather of all advertising media, print. Print media has been around since businesses began advertising their wares and services. Print media, i.e., coupons, newsprint, postcards, etc., are practically ineffective today.

There are the mediums of email marketing and text message marketing. Email marketing has become the assumed medium to reach consumers. Email marketing is inexpensive and when done according to the CAN-SPAM laws email marketing can be reasonably effective. The real downside to email marketing is that even when consumers opt-in they don't check their email when received thus the risk of your marketing piece going stale resulting in positive minimal responses.

Finally to get immediate, measurable results with full control over your marketing and advertising campaigns there is the 21st century new media, "text message marketing." Text message marketing puts your advertisement in the hands of your target market within seconds of sending it. The message is delivered to the smartphones of your opt-in customer base. Text message marketing is extremely affordable, measurable and flexible. If you have the campaign to increase traffic, you can do it within minutes with text message marketing. Statistics show that on average text messages are read within 4 minutes of being received. Another great benefit of text message marketing is that you can choose to do it yourself or have a text message marketing company handle the marketing campaigns for you. You simply submit your campaign to the text message marketing company, and they handle the setup and transmission of your campaign based upon your directions, even to the minute of transmission.

**Thank you for purchasing and taking time to read this book. I hope it has answered all your questions!**